CW01209433

The Adventures of Asva in Istanbul

Niyati Goel

TRAVELLING TOES

Copyright © 2023 by Niyati Goel

All rights reserved.

TRAVELLINGTOES21CENTURY

We are off to Turkey!

At only seven years old, Asva had already seen more of the world than many adults. Gifted with wanderlust, he learned to walk by pushing his feet across train platforms and cobblestone streets. His parents were travel bloggers, and their love affair with adventure began before he was even born. Now, their mission was to share all the places they cherished, and those they were yet to discover, with their intrepid little explorer.

And so began the adventures of Asva.

It was September, and the air was cool in Asva's hometown, Oslo, Norway. The trees were just starting to show their autumn colors. The leaves were turning from bright green to deep red. His parents always said that this was their favorite time to go on vacation, when the summer crowds had disappeared and all the flights and trains were less packed.

The long-awaited journey was upon them, and it would be to Istanbul! The city of Djinns and magical adventures. Asva felt a thrill run through him that made his fingers tingle. Packing had become an adventure with mom and dad, both experienced travelers who knew how to make the pre-vacation period even more fun. He imagined all sorts of magical things like in his favorite movie, Chronicles of Narnia. He couldn't wait to try the most delicious Turkish delights every single day during their stay in Istanbul.

Asva's excitement was at its peak as he settled himself in between his parents on the airplane. He wanted to make sure that he could keep an eye on both of them, and with luck, he'd also be able to sit in front of the window. Sure enough, when the time came for takeoff, Asva had a straight view out the window - it was magical!

After dinner, Asva felt cozy and safe, snuggled up between his mom and dad as the plane sped through the air. Soon enough, he drifted off into dreamland, ready for his escapades in Istanbul. Little did he know, his journey would be much more adventurous than he ever imagined in his wildest dreams!

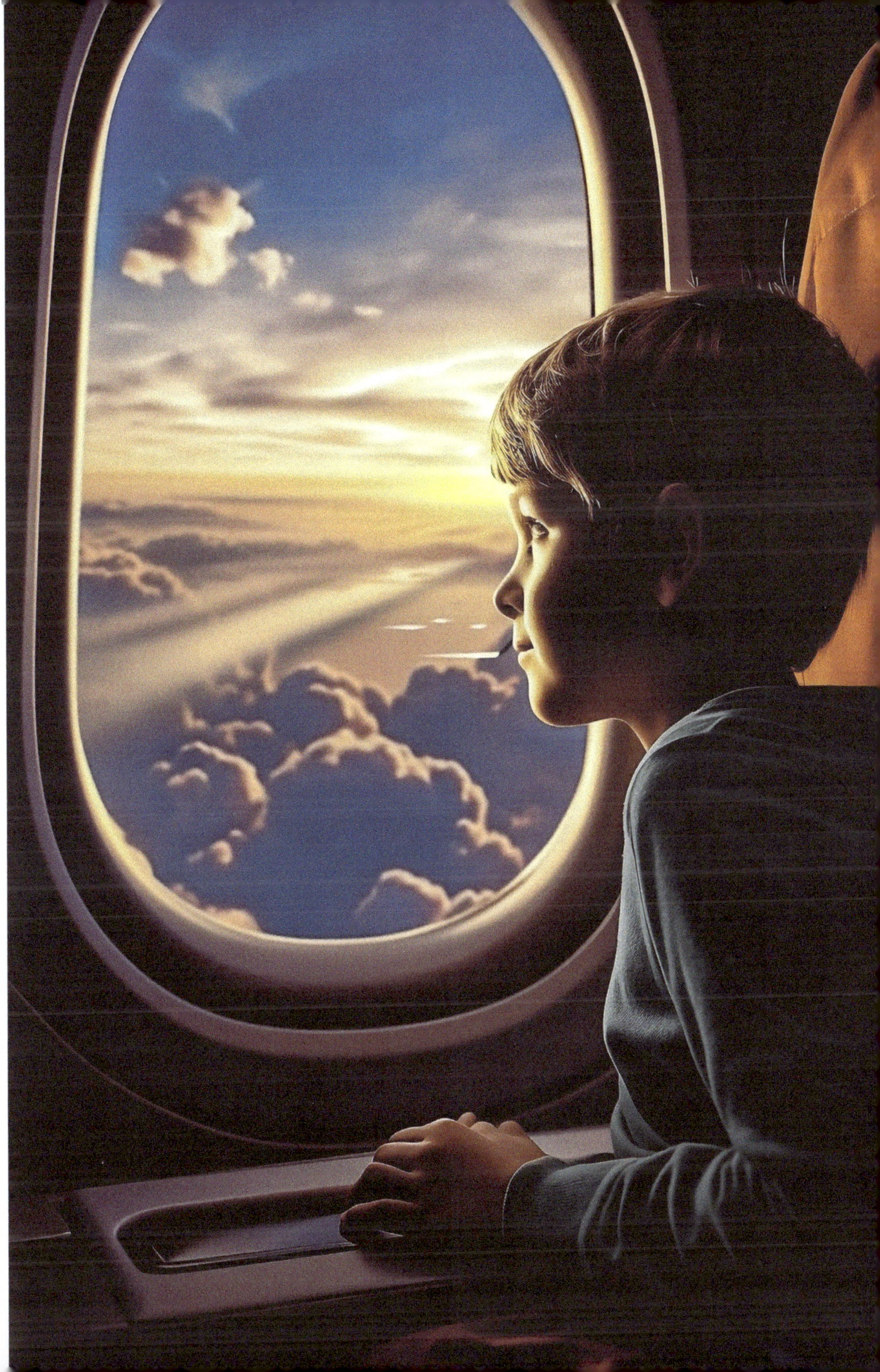

The family flew to Istanbul in the night. When they got to the hotel, they were so tired from the trip that they dived right into bed to get some rest. As morning came, they were awakened by unfamiliar sounds coming from outside. It wasn't the chirping of the birds like back home, but a loud noise that seemed to echo throughout the city , 'Azaan' the call to prayer! Cars and people filled the streets, all buzzing with excitement for what the new day would bring. With eyes wide open, Asva was the first one up to see this brand new place.

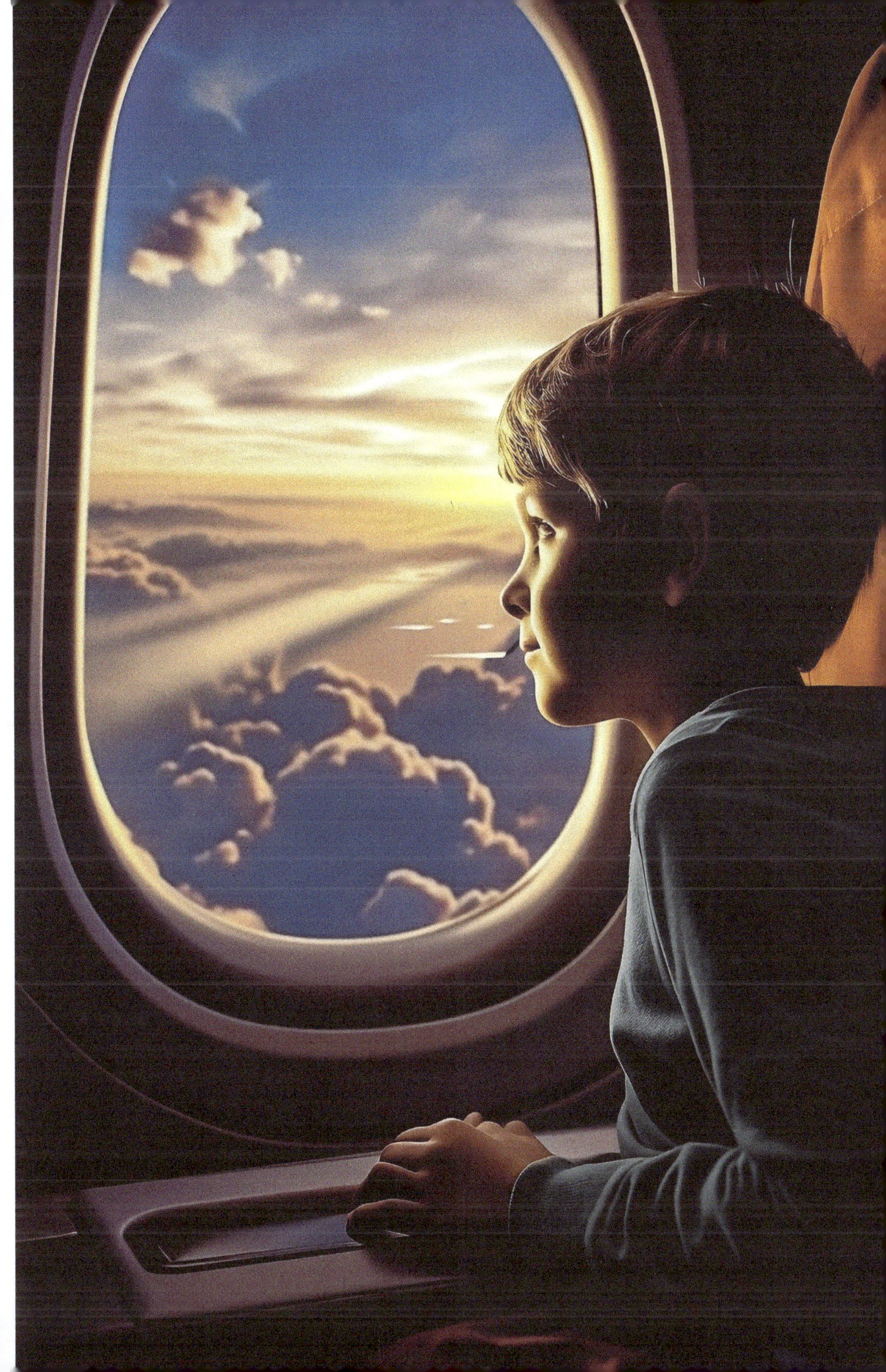

The family flew to Istanbul in the night. When they got to the hotel, they were so tired from the trip that they dived right into bed to get some rest. As morning came, they were awakened by unfamiliar sounds coming from outside. It wasn't the chirping of the birds like back home, but a loud noise that seemed to echo throughout the city , 'Azaan' the call to prayer! Cars and people filled the streets, all buzzing with excitement for what the new day would bring. With eyes wide open, Asva was the first one up to see this brand new place.

He was filled with energy. Today, he was finally going to take his first ever cruise across the Bosphorus Strait! His parents had told him about it, and he had learned in school that it split Istanbul between the continents of Asia and Europe. But first, they were going to explore Taksim Square – all the fun things his parents had mentioned about it made him even more eager to get started.

As the golden morning sun peeked out from behind the mountains, Asva and his parents got ready for an exciting day at Taksim Square. Everywhere they looked was a new experience! They could smell all sorts of delicious food cooking in the restaurants, hear vendors calling out their wares, watch busy tour guides gather groups of visitors, listen to boats announcing departure times, and the red tram's screeching wheels turn the corner.

But first, it was time to grab a bite to eat- they had a delicious breakfast which consisted of Turkish coffee, fluffy bread covered in roasted tomatoes, and baklava - a special treat made of nuts and honey that practically melted in your mouth. Once they finished their meal, they set off around the square in anticipation of their day ahead.

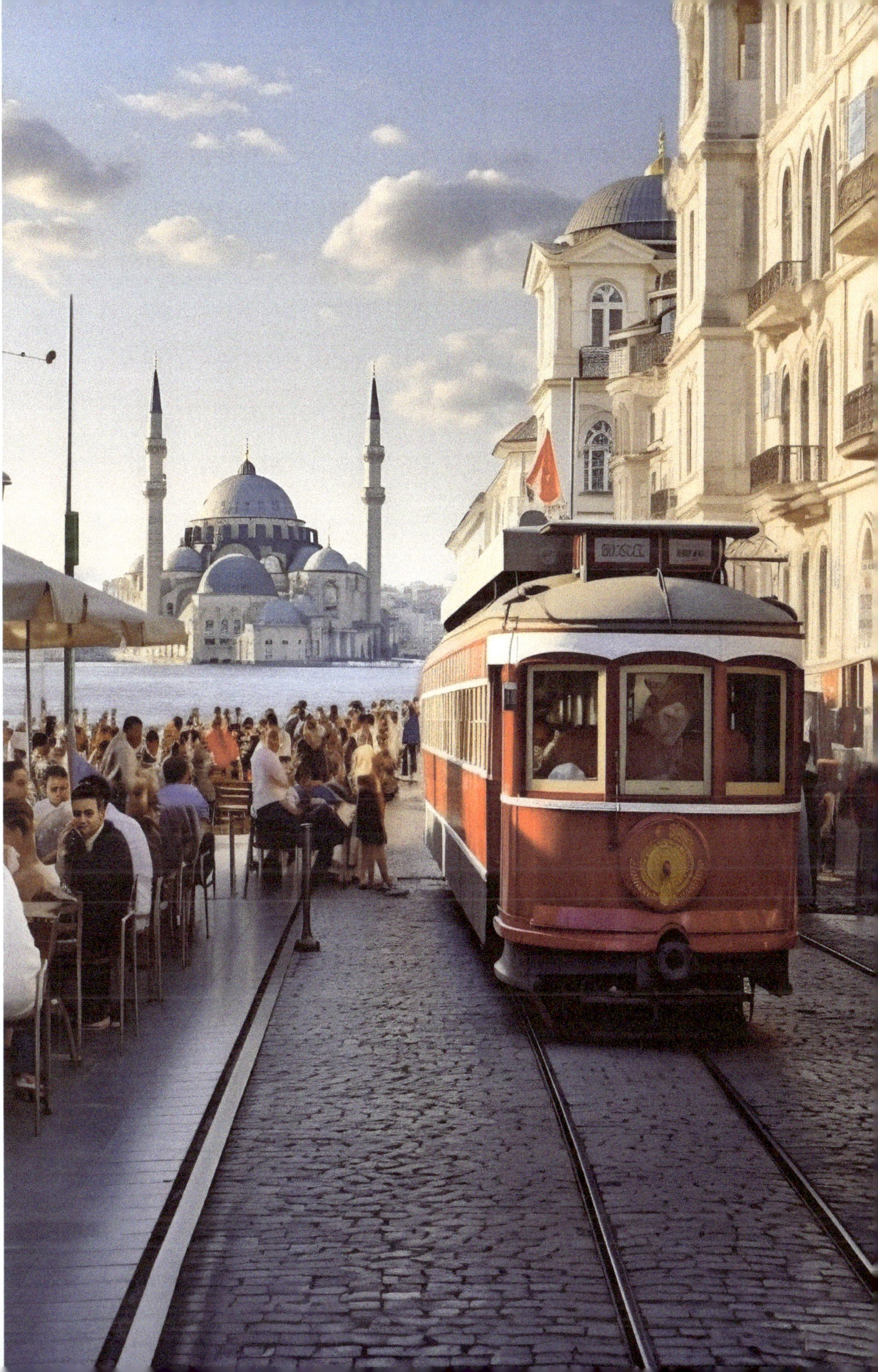

Asva's eyes lit up when he saw a caricature artist drawing colorful portraits of a mother and son sitting opposite him. He knew that something similar would be the perfect thing to hang on his bedroom wall back in Oslo. Meanwhile, his mom took some time to browse around the antique shops, and his dad stayed behind to monitor the progress of the portrait.

Just as the artist had finished putting on the final strokes on Asva's caricature, their tour guide for the day, Cemil, arrived with his son Ruslan in tow. After quickly rolling up his new piece of art, Asva ran over to meet Cemil and Ruslan for the first time since their video call earlier in the week.

Ruslan was the same age as Asva, and shared his enthusiasm for adventure. Ruslan had lived in Istanbul for most of his life, and knew the place quite well.

Asva was looking forward to the rest of the day, which promised a cruise on the Bosphorus, an exploration of the city in the afternoon, and a night devoted to savoring Mezze dishes and watching the Whirling Dervishes. However, little did he know the events he would experience that day would surpass even his wildest imagination!

The Spirit of Bosphorus

He couldn't contain his excitement as he stepped onto the cruise boat. The wind brushed against his face, and the bobbing of the boat on the waves below made him feel as though he was truly setting off on an adventure. The sweet smell of hot chocolate wafted up from where the crew was serving refreshments.

Asva and his new friend Ruslan stood at the deck with their parents watching them. Cemil spoke in the background about how one side of the river offered a view of Asia's monuments and cultural sites, and the other was lined with Europe's architectural wonders.

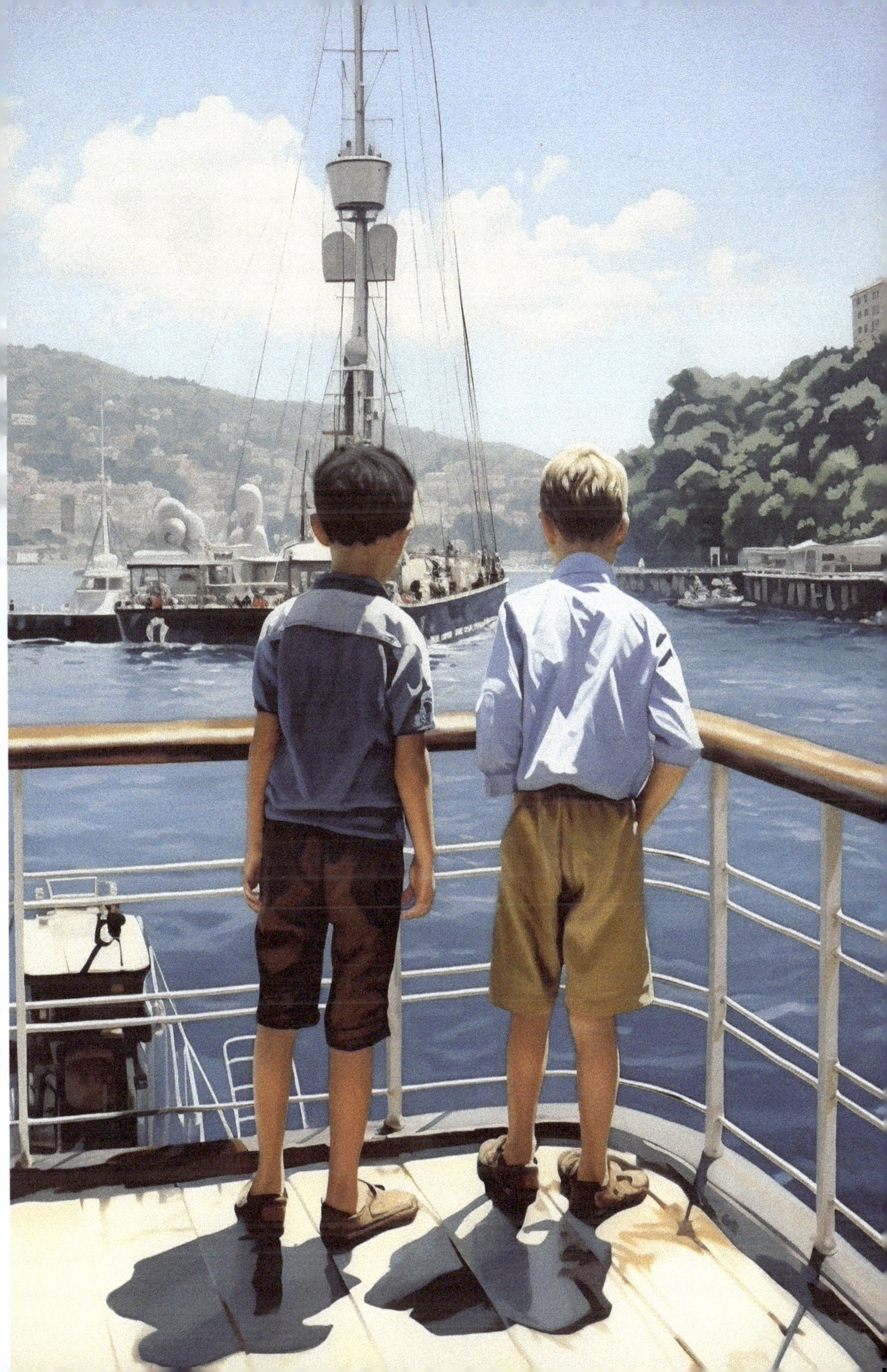

Asva and Ruslan squealed in delight when they felt the cool spray of water on their faces. Just then, a girl a little younger than them approached them. She had beautiful dark skin, black hair, and was wearing a brown top and a skirt. She softly said Hello to Asva and Ruslan before asking if they wanted to go inside the cruise cabin to chat. Asva thought for a bit, then asked his mother if this was okay; and she gave her approval. Asva, Ruslan, and the mysterious girl named Zehra occupied some empty seats inside the cabin. Then Zehra said something so incredible that Asva thought she was pranking them!

She told them that she had been lost for months. She hadn't seen her parents since they'd sailed on this very boat on the Bosphorus one summer morning. Everyday she saw people come and go but it wasn't her parents. Where were her parents and older brother? Had they forgotten all about her?

As Asva and Ruslan were talking to her, Asva's mom came over bearing cookies—except she only gave one to each of them. Asva thought it was rude of his mother not to share and asked, "Mum, can you give Zehra one too?" His mother stopped and looked at him quizzically, asking "Who, Asva? Who is Zehra and where is she?" Even though they were young, Asva and Ruslan both realised no one else could see her. They let the moment pass in silence. Asva knew something strange was going on, and then they asked Zehra who she was.

Zehra let out a heavy sigh, realizing she would have to explain to them that she was a lost spirit who could not leave this cruise. She had been stuck here for what felt like ages, missing her family terribly. She had tried talking to all the people who got onboard the cruise, but no one responded to her 'hello' until now; someone was finally willing to chat with her. She remembered what her mother had taught her: keep trying and you will eventually find someone who can hear you.

As it turned out, it was two young boys who were truly listening with their hearts who ultimately heard her.

Now that Asva had recovered from the surprise and Ruslan was by his side, he wanted to know more. What could they do to cheer Zehra up? All she wished for in this world was to see her mom and dad and older brother again. "Who are your parents? Where do they live? Would they come if we go to them?" he asked. Zehra, however, had no answers. Her mum and dad were all she knew; they lived in Istanbul in a bustling area, where noises of cars and street vendors filled the air and there was a large carpet store overlooking the living room window. Asva felt her pain – he wanted to locate her parents badly, but the problem was that what she described resembled most of Istanbul. Even if he managed it, how would he explain it all to his parents who couldn't even see Zehra?

He made a mental note of all the information Zehra shared and promised her that he would bring her family on the cruise soon. He and Ruslan then brainstormed, scarcely paying attention to wherever they were going with their parents. They had some great plans; Ruslan was a local in Istanbul afterall, and he knew, based on Zehra's description, where they should start searching.

She had mentioned that every Sunday morning her mom would take her and her brother to the Grand Bazaar of Istanbul at a specific shop, where the shopkeeper always gave the two kids two pieces of Turkish Delight of their choice! She used to pick the pomegranate and pistachio ones while her brother always chose two almond Turkish delights. The name of the store was peculiar but she didn't recall it - she only remembered that they initially found it by grabbing a flyer at Hagia Sophia Mosque. The flyer was bright red in color and stood out from others.

The Hunt Begins

Hagia Sophia Mosque was on the itinerary for the day; it was an unmissable point of interest for anyone who came to Istanbul. Cemil explained to them, this architectural wonder was a living relic of the time when Islam and Christianity coexisted peacefully.

Once they were inside, they saw that the ceiling overhead was pure stained glass, the sun shining through them, bathing the whole building in warm colors. The air smelled of burning beeswax, incense, and a hint of rose water. The dull hum of a thousand people, the chants, the prayers, and the shuffling feet was the most amazing experience that gave Asva goosebumps.

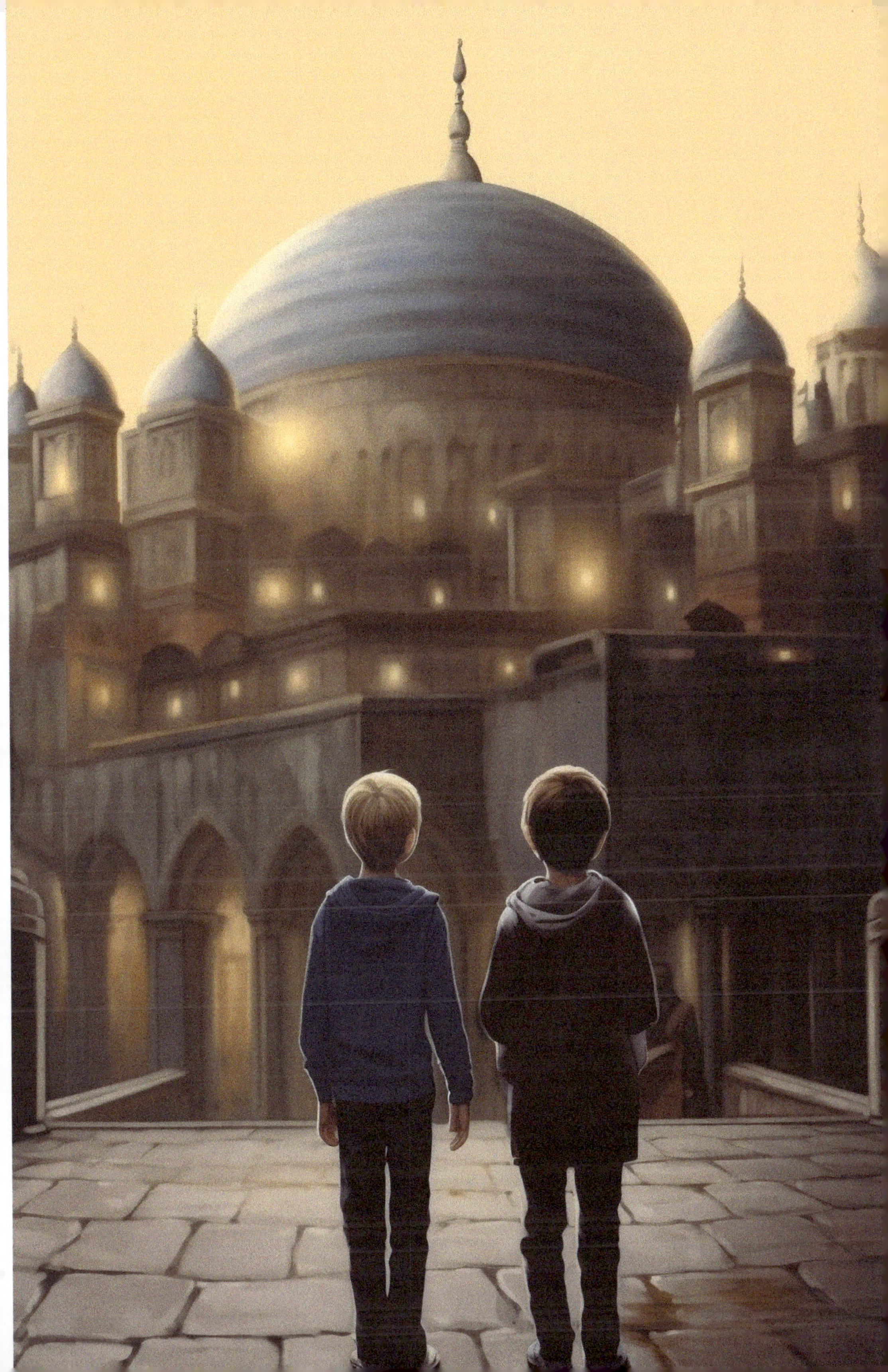

It was in these surroundings they had to find the flyer box while their parents chatted about the historical significance of the mosque.

Asva and Ruslan asked their parents if they could look around the Hagia Sophia. They ran past the security guard's chair, the water fountain, and the restrooms, until they reached a stand near the entrance. It was full of colorful flyers - greens and pinks, blues and red. From all of them, only one stood out from the rest- it was deep red all over and matched Zehra's description! That had to be one - it said in large font 'Sultan's Delight! at the Grand Bazaar Istanbul' - a shop filled with all sorts of amazing sweets and Turkish delights among its many treats.

That was step one. Next stop would be the Grand Bazaar, another amazing place to continue their adventure.

The bazaar was a massive maze of market stalls and shops, all lit by the hanging lights and street lamps that were outside. Every direction from the entrance felt like a different world. From the chaotic and colorful clothes shops, to the kitchenware stalls, to the carpet stalls to the Turkish delight shops, there was a never-ending labyrinth of exotic smells, sights, and sounds. No one could find their way here without a guide on their first visit.

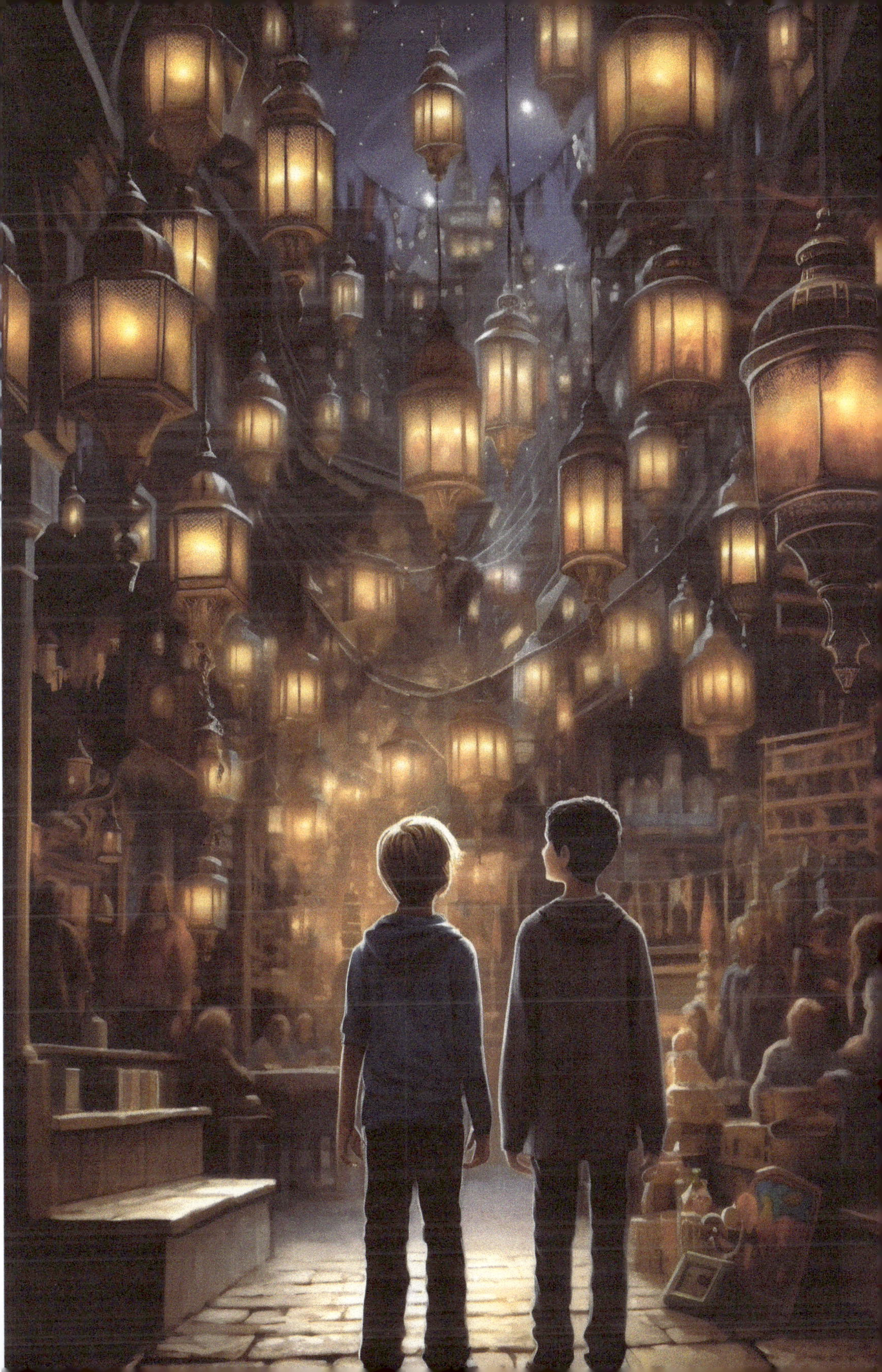

But Ruslan was a mini guide himself and could locate the section of the Istanbul Grand Bazaar that sold sweet treats, cutting down their search time. The friends were able to pick up at least a few pieces of Turkish delights from each shop before they had to get back to their parents at the entrance in less than thirty minutes. Asva's father had taken the extra initiative to ensure his pocket was loaded with a charged cell phone along with a location tracker every day before they left their hotel while on vacation.

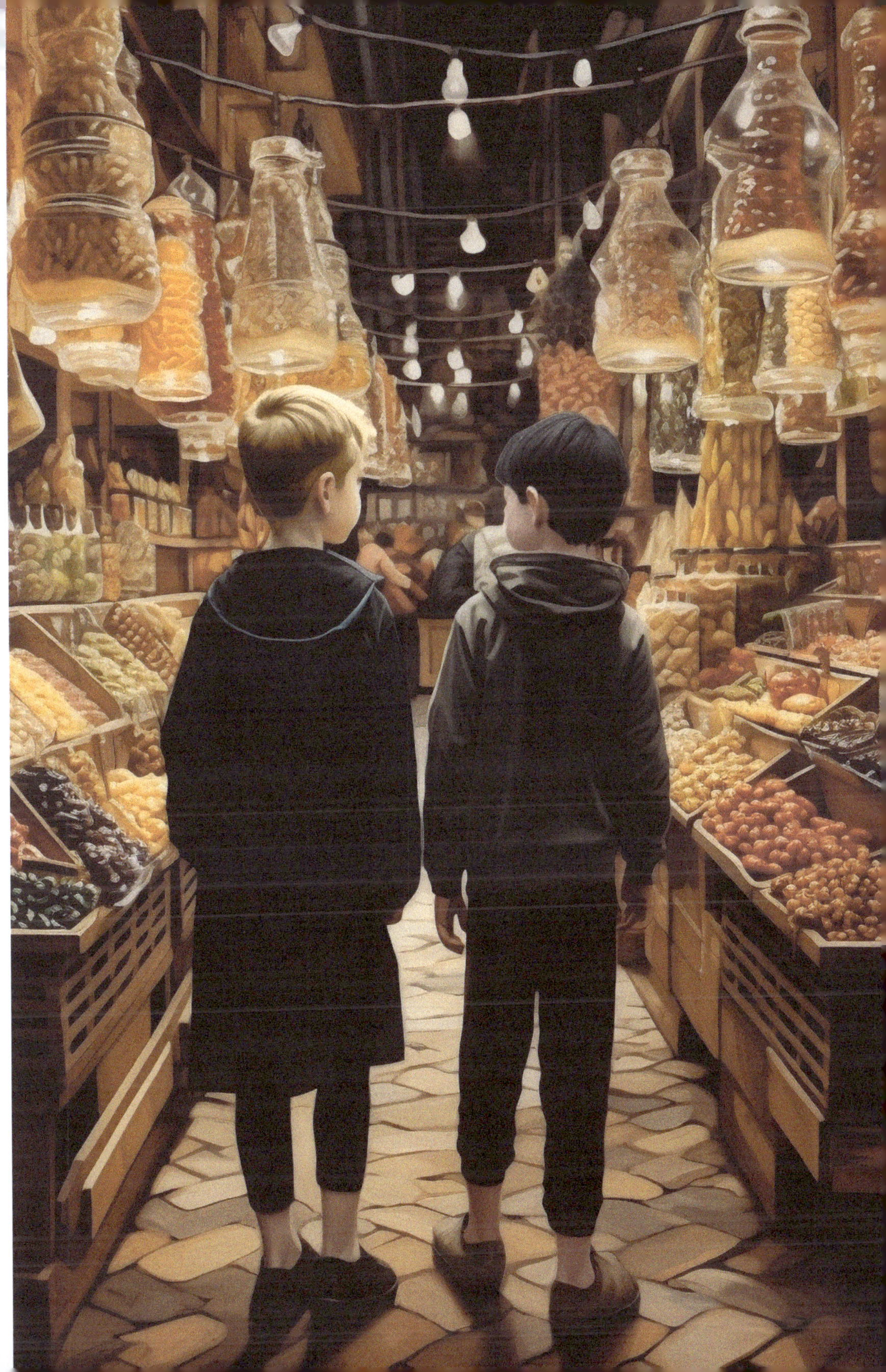

After indulging in more than 20 different kinds of Turkish Delights, they knew they had finally arrived at the right place when they saw the sign for Sultan's Delight! Excitedly, they told the shopkeeper all about Zehra, a little girl who used to come with her family to the shop every Sunday. While her mom bought household groceries, she could pick out whatever type of Turkish delight she wanted and so would her brother.

The shopkeeper smiled as he remembered this happy family who would visit their store week after week until one day, around a year ago, they stopped coming. He recalled that they lived in a neighborhood not too far from the Galata Tower where Zehra's dad owned a carpet shop. That was all he knew!

So it was up to Asva and Ruslan to locate Zehra's parents. They managed to persuade their parents to accompany them that afternoon to Galata tower, where they intended to search for either Zehra's house or her father's shop. It was clear that tracking down the house with only the description of its orange color and two floors above ground would be a nearly impossible task, as there were simply too many doors to knock on. Finding the unnamed carpet shop might be less difficult, but it could still prove to be a challenge.

They traveled along the street full of carpet shops, each time waiting until the shopkeeper was free of customers before they could approach and inquire about Zehra. After five attempts of this, both Asva and Ruslan were exhausted.

At last, in a store situated at the corner of the road, next to a pile of tattered carpets kept in a basket, they shouted out for the shopkeeper who couldn't be seen. Eventually, a man emerged and shook hands with the two boys. His hands were soft and wrinkled and he wore a ring with an image resembling little Zehra. Ruslan stepped forward and told him about Zehra. Upon hearing her name he practically fainted and had to catch himself just in time.

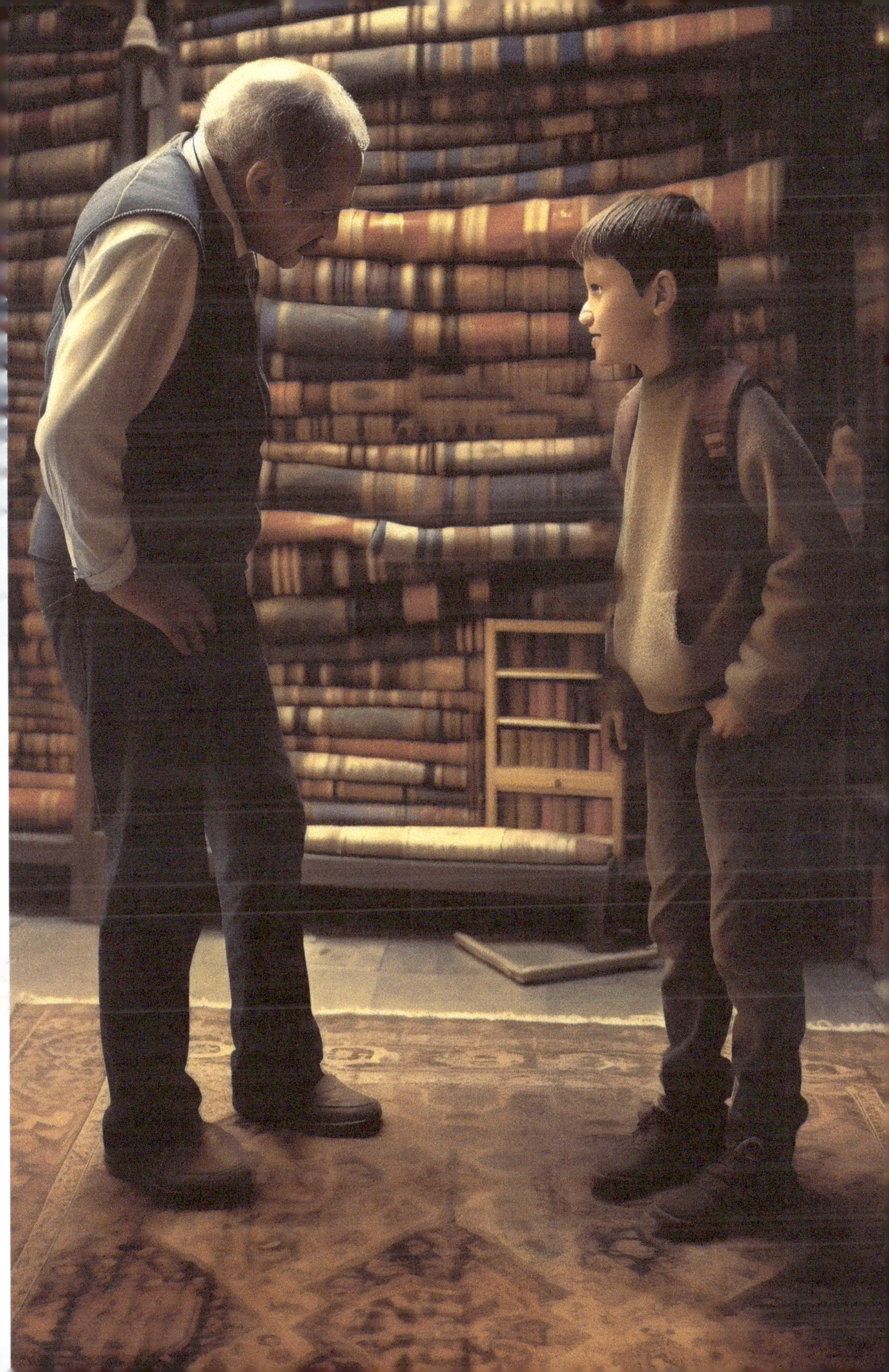

The shopkeeper questioned Asva and Ruslan for more information about his daughter. When he was convinced they had the correct details, he raced home with the two boys in tow. Meanwhile, Asva had contacted his father to inform him they'd be a bit late in getting to the cafe. Although it was strange to get that call, his parents knew he and Ruslan were alright, as long as Asva kept checking in every hour or so, since they had led a bold life of travel blogging themselves.

When they arrived at Zehra's house, they heard her mother scream. She emerged and began to ask them questions - it was hard to believe two young boys had spoken to her daughter's spirit earlier that day. When she was thoroughly convinced, the couple got in their car and asked Asva and Ruslan to join them. The boys didn't want to miss a second of the adventure, so they jumped into the vehicle and Zehra's father drove straight ahead towards their son's school to pick him up as well.

On the ride, Zehra's mother told them about a trip they took on the Bosphorus cruise boat last summer. When no one was looking, Zehra and her brother had climbed onto the railing of the boat in excitement. Suddenly, a wave splashed against the side of the boat and in that moment, Zehra lost her grip and dropped into the deep water below. Her brother managed to keep his footing until he opened his eyes again and noticed that Zehra had disappeared.

He started calling out her name desperately, but it was too late -- she was already gone. Several other people had also been soaked from head to toe, with some even losing their phones or purses in the commotion. Zehra's brother ran inside to get their parents while the crew searched for her aboard the ship. But after thirty minutes of searching, there was still no sign of her.

The police were eventually called and a search party of divers went out on the Bosphorus Strait with only a route map of where the boat had been to guide them.

Four hours after sending out the search party, they returned to Taksim square empty-handed. It had been the toughest day of their lives, and yet they kept coming back to the same location in case Zehra somehow managed to find her way back home. Even though deep down they knew she was gone, there remained a tiny hope that maybe she could be found alive.

An Anticipated Reunion

Today, the family came together to say goodbye to their daughter for the final time, even though she was only a spirit. After picking up her brother, who was only slightly older than Zehra, they went to the cruise boat station in Taksim Square and bought five tickets.

They all settled in a corner of the deck that was usually vacant and waited for the boat to depart. Taking deep breaths, Asva and Ruslan wondered if Zehra would show up. The cruise started towards the Bosphorus Strait between the Black Sea and Mediterranean, but as everyone started to worry, Zehra appeared right in front of them.

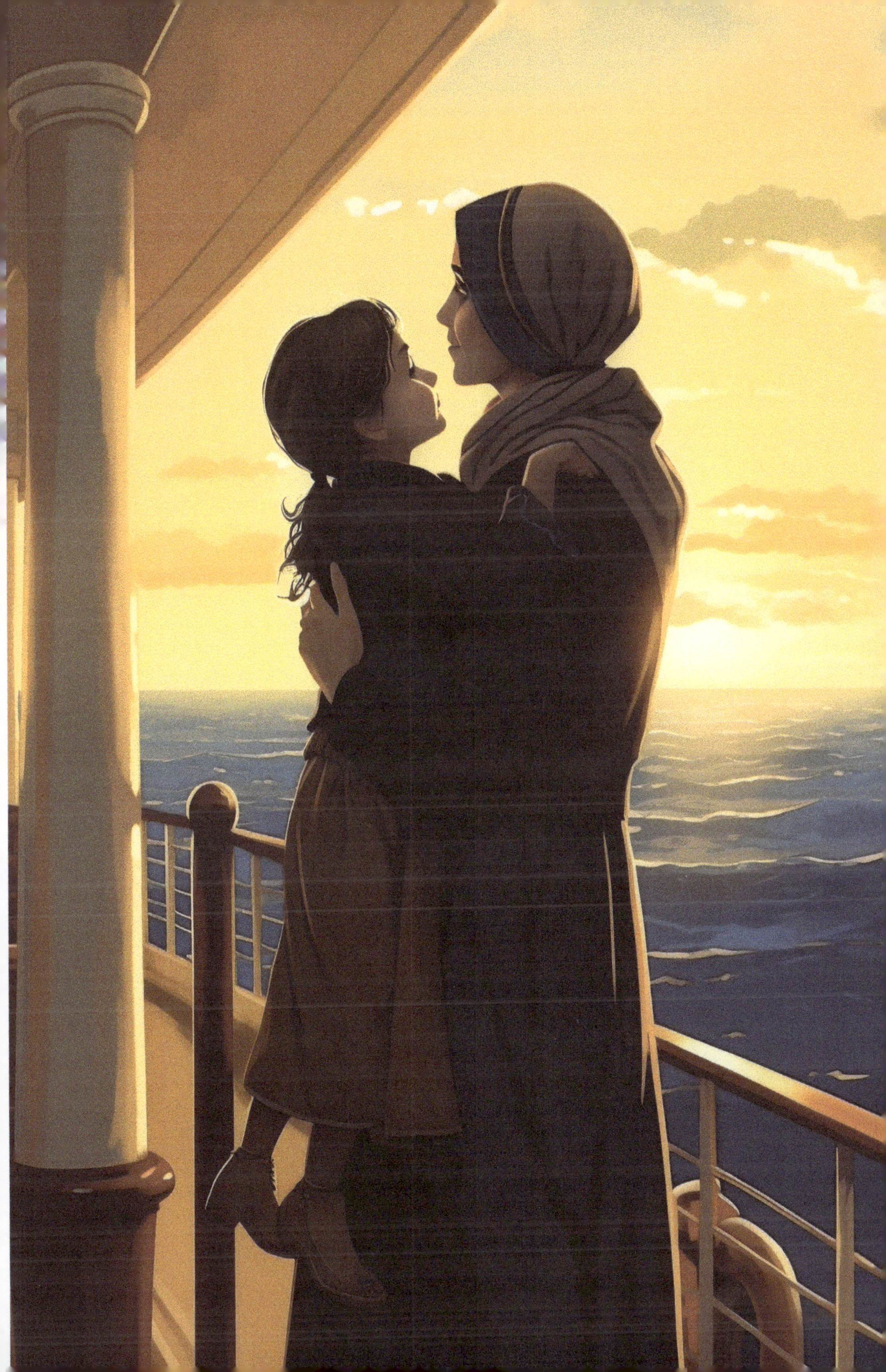

No one could speak at first, until Zehra's sweet voice broke through their shock and tears began rolling down her cheeks. Fortunately, most passengers were inside the cabin leaving the deck almost deserted, giving Zehra and her family a moment to cry, hug, talk, and express their grief. They thanked the boys for providing them with this chance for closure.

After half-hour of intense emotions, Zehra's figure began to fade from Asva's sight - he rubbed his eyes in disbelief, but it didn't make any difference; she was really vanishing. Her parents and brother said their goodbyes, tearfully and with smiles. With her head bowed slightly, Zehra disappeared. Asva watched as her beloved family spent the last moments of the cruise holding onto one another and weeping in gratitude for being able to let her go.

Just before the boat returned to the dock, Asva's phone started ringing. He managed to answer on the third ring and heard his father asking what he wanted from the cafe near Galata Tower, where they were already seated for a late lunch. Such an everyday inquiry felt oddly trivial after what he'd just lived through. He mumbled something about bread and baklava before hanging up. When they arrived back on dry land, Zehra's family embraced Asva and Ruslan while giving them their contact information and inviting them over for dinner that same week. Overcome with tears, Asva quickly looked away; but when his gaze met Ruslan's, they shared a silent moment of pride in their friendship – strengthened by this unforgettable day.

The taxi made its way back to the Galata Tower district, where their parents were already seated at the cafe. As soon as Asva and Ruslan stepped inside, they were warmly welcomed. The smell of fresh bread, salad, pumpkin soup and a chickpea dish made them realize just how hungry they were! After scarfing down their food, they knew what the other was thinking but they weren't ready to share their adventures with anyone yet. So, without saying a word, they sat in contentment during dessert. They both looked forward to the evening's Whirling Dervishes show; it would be another story altogether.

Author Bio

Currently residing in San Francisco with her husband, Niyati, a passionate traveler, has explored over 21 countries, traversing continents and collecting incredible adventures along the way. Her love for solo backpacking is only rivaled by her dedication to her full-time career.

While Niyati's heart belongs to exploration, it also finds solace in the pages of books, with her earliest literary love being Ayn Rand. Now, she's embarking on a new chapter as a first-time author, aiming to bridge her passion for travel and literature in a way that promises to captivate and inspire readers worldwide.